HIGH GROUND COWARD

Winner of the Iowa Poetry Prize

HIGH GROUND COWARD

▲▲▲

POEMS BY ALICIA MOUNTAIN

University of Iowa Press, Iowa City

University of Iowa Press, Iowa City 52242

Copyright © 2018 by Alicia Mountain

www.uipress.uiowa.edu

Printed in the United States of America

Design by Ashley Muehlbauer

The University of Iowa Press is a member of Green Press
Initiative and is committed to preserving natural resources.

Printed on acid-free paper

Library of Congress Cataloging-in-Publication Data

Names: Mountain, Alicia, author.

Title: High ground coward / Alicia Mountain.

Description: Iowa City : University Of Iowa Press, [2018] |
Series: Iowa Poetry Prize

Identifiers: LCCN 2017039374 (print) | LCCN 2017051329
(e-book) | ISBN 978-1-60938-545-3 (paperback : acid-free
paper) | ISBN 978-1-60938-546-0 (e-book)

Subjects: BISAC: POETRY / General.

Classification: LCC PS3613.O857 (e-book) | LCC PS3613.O857
A6 2018 (print) | DDC 811/.6—dc23

LC record available at https://lccn.loc.gov/2017039374

For my parents,
with love.

CONTENTS

No one
to witness
and adjust, no one to drive the car

—WILLIAM CARLOS WILLIAMS

HIGH GROUND COWARD

THE BOOK IS A HUNGRY DARKNESS

My desires are berries because they are small and many.
Fig leaves embarrass the body.
Wine is my water when I am writing,

blood when I am dancing, sweating.

My parents' god is the sun
at 7 A.M. in December, that close to nothing.

My father had no sons.
My mother sends my wife her love.
In all of this, forgiveness

assumes sin and I'm not sorry.

I am the snake and I am the silence,
an animal's rib picked clean.

DEADBOLT DOOR SYNDROME

There are ghosts in the crawl space that hold us
like a mother. They say any heavy footfall
sounds angry when it's above your head.

Authority is more afraid than you are,
there is no blood that breaks you.

If the research studied scare tactics and shame
we'd know why, when the drugs don't work,
I steal a red Sharpie from Rite Aid
and write *fagz run this town* on walls
in plain view, thinking no one is watching.
That way we are everywhere indelible.

To be sure, to be clear, I wasn't
even alive when this started. Who am I
to carry loss like a back pocket flag?

And I don't have an answer,
except that this is a most inherited part:
a vestigial light in the hiding places,
a book of matches struck all at once.

THE SMALLEST THAW

During the bleak week that straddled
November and December I became reliant
on potting soil. I kept forty pounds
in my trunk as a more hopeful sandbag.
When that weight was not enough
and my tires, even with their studs,
spun like a stomping bull at slaughter,
I cut the thing open and shook
clean soil into the white piled street.

I left a bottle of red wine in the trunk
overnight, not thinking. With the expansive
cold the cork crawled out through the foil,
wine seeped into the dirt that spilled
from the gutted bag. The rest froze solid,
sideways—a phantom ship in a bottle.

Driving to work, the smell of dirt said
you are not going to the rented office clinic,
you are going to your grandfather's field.
This wasn't true. But after my clients,
I fishtailed my way to the first farm
I could find. A Montana tundra farm
outside of town, quiet, well chewed at

by two swollen goats. I tromped out to
a break in the snow where a barn had been
razed to its foundation and crouched
by the iced-over ground for a while.

When the unwelcome snow in my boots
began to melt against my pale ankles,
I stood and turned to walk back.
I opened the trunk, put my hands into
that dark. My fists grabbed on as if
it was something that could hold me.

DRIVE THRU

Franchise French fries
and a Frosty
in the front seat chill of January—
　　all I need is the swamp of you.
And to speak
with the backlit voice
through an intercom
in unhurried tones of decision,
　　though I know what I want.
Static seasoning
the breath between us
　　as if we are far apart
　　as if I am calling
　　from a submarine at peacetime
　　　and the crew is happy
　　　but they miss their mothers—
　　　they have waited months
　　　for the mail to come.

Because of my mom
we went to Wendy's.
Because Dave Thomas
was adopted as a baby,

before going on to found Wendy's
we went to Wendy's.
Because my mom was an orphan too
we went to Wendy's,
     which is notable
     for using fresh (not frozen)
     ground beef in square patties
     that hang over the edge of
     a round bun.
And I don't eat burgers anymore
but there is a square-peg-round-hole
phenomenon for each of us.

     There is a Dave Thomas for each of us.

My father quit ROTC
and says it's his great regret.
Dave Thomas quit high school
and learned to cook
in the Korean War.
Before I was 18
my father never asked
and I never told
until someone
     in the crepe paper dark
     of a dorm room
sighed and said,
     all your desires are sacred.

What a way to fall in love with wanting.

Tonight I am asking for
    hot and cold
    for grease and sweet
    somewhere between chocolate and putty
    a mouth up against a milk carton
    froth the color of gray matter,
        a bit purple
        a brain frozen
        a brain freeze.

Please.

The sentry in his sentry box
is not so far away.
And what he means to say is not
    pull up to the window

but rather,
    come up for air,
        you submarine,
        you draft dodger,
        you twilight party of one.

    All your desires are sacred.
    All you need is to speak them aloud.

ON BEING TOLD TO DO WHATEVER I WANT

Whatever I want is to run the stick of my deodorant
along each of your spread-eagle limbs
to dig my nails into your forearm at takeoff
and find turbulence every time
and be afraid of nothing and falling
to split a cake for dinner
or light the sheets on fire
to take a raccoon as a pet
train it to fold more tiny paper raccoons with its little human hands
to make twins of each of us
watch them braid each other's hair
watch them use their tongues
to know for certain we will die at night
to know which commodities you've stolen
and convince the hygienist I'm committed to flossing
to wipe away the lint stuck to my lips.
What I want has been crouched so long it cannot stand
it is filament
it is hardware store
it is someday I'll sharpen the knives
the skim milk of your belly and back.
I want leftovers for breakfast
want you gentle and heathen
I want to talk like a preacher in your bathrobe

to embarrass myself before company
until you paint my face a disguise
and call your mother
and hear her breathe on the phone
and hang up
and owe nothing to the bank
and the twins of us are in love
but won't say it
and the sound of their sleeping is ice melting in a jar.

ELYSIAN / ECHO

the park in Echo Park
is called Elysian

with steps so steep
we couldn't speak

pebbles before becoming
a rockslide

half of me
holding out a hand

to keep you
my own cold plum

I would buy you
things I can't afford

an orchard emptied
from the storm

the tail of a meteor
you thought you saw

someone like me
but more true

I watched you
even after you said

don't watch me
while I fall

SOUTHPAW SKIN THE GLOVES

The coroner's children are fat
in a happy way.

Not in a KwikMart way,
where my entourage is a bench
in the sun and more than one man
tells me the bus doesn't run
here anymore.

But the one who stops and squints with me says,

I watched Boom Boom Mancini
kill a man in the ring
watched it live,   on TV,   TV-live.

Saw the punch that laid him into the ropes,
put him in a coma,
put him in the ground.

I was a kid and it ruined me,
I still see it.

Even the ref
killed himself after
he didn't stop the fight.

SUCCESSION PLANTING

In raised beds we unfamine
    our little rectangular earths.

                        Foot-apart three-seed clusters
                          we plan on forgetting to thin.

Sunscreen break.
Kissing break.
Rosé break, that my friend calls
    some white lady shit.

                  How to make *right-now* Vitamin D
                  without the harvest promise part?

Borrowing sunglasses was neither
    answer nor anxiety.

          But sleep-cool in the basement I'll dream a clean hand
               pushing them up my greasy forehead.

I'll dream a kissing break awake,
    tearing another month from the calendar.

NPR in the kitchen and a woman who is impressed
    every time I make the salad dressing.

Who could blame a lonely mower?
Who hasn't done slow growing?

Nothing against the garden.
Nothing against the weeds therein.

Disarray knows how to bide its time.

HAYMAKER BARNBURNER

And so the spotlit Fight of the Century
starts slowly—
timid tapping airborne hands

like featherweight bees
bobbing between
apricot tree and apple.

All this, the work of a singular bounty,
the out-of-reach hound crowd,
their howling sound.

Surveil and surveil and survive,

keep alive by footwork
that writes   l u n g e—   and retreat
                     l u n g e—   and retreat

In capitol, in seminary, in extant sundown town
whose fist is raised?
Whose liver-spotted hand smears ointment in the corner?

SAFETY OFF

There is a shooter   in the mall where she works.
She hasn't seen him yet   but customers are running
down the escalators in shrieks, becoming so fleshy

                                        as they move.

She is the narrator, Jules tells me.
Walkie-talkies describe a gunman who is unmistakably
her angry angry stupid brother   lonely.

I am lazy. I don't even ask if his rampage brain
consummates what it set out to do.   Or I can't bear
that she put that kind of violence through skinny fingers.

Jules asks, *should I write the ending so that the sister*
                                        finds out he survives
or so that we don't know what happens to him?

She won't have the brother die, in the story.   I am disappointed.
    What is *wrong* with me that I want that?

I wait in my car outside her house,
                    because it had seemed still too much winter to walk
to the movie—   which was very good.   It won an award.

For a week I tell anyone I like that it was
              fight club and *black swan* and *eternal sunshine* put together—

On the street afterwards, I offer Caylin a ride too.
We let the car warm, watch a woman rehearse ballet in her kitchen.
        She moves like practice, elbows in,
              just gesturing the turns and leaps,
          her back to the window.

Caylin says we will all have sugarplum fairies
in apartments in our poems.
                  But I call dibs and Jules says dibs is real.

We spend a driveway half hour telling Caylin
    how to go on a date   as if we know.
She asks if she should wear an all black outfit
        to the funeral we're going to on Thursday,
which is before her date,   which would be totally fine
              because she looks good in black.

We say don't text the guy that   *those fries are the bomb dot gov.*
She goes with *those fries are insanely good*   and tells us she loves us
and squeals
    and slams the car door
      and prances through the back-porch dark—

We have only a few blocks left to drive.   I tell Jules
    the narrator should find out her brother lives—
it would be the more terrible outcome,
                    the rest of *that* life.

You are so sinister, she says, undoing her seatbelt.

Should I leave it open-ended here?
Or write that she kisses me hard on the mouth,
              the more unbearable thing.

THE WHOLE WATER-FACED AUDITORIUM
for C. D. Wright

Body exalt.
Ozarks exalt.
Judge and court reporter and shorthand exalt.

Salt the ice where the grave-pull hits you.

The porch hammer guard-dogs what we've got,

    champagne taste
    and high life money.

White girls fuck white girls without drawing the blinds.
Sometimes light bulbs fall asleep, too.

There is no sell by date on mourning.

ALMANAC TRACTION

The end of this year is a congealing cold gravy
in every kitchen I know. A mountain pass
you can't legally cross without chains.
And I can't help dwelling on the unenforcement of this
and the cost of chains,   the daymare of rolling over.
                              And then who would water the plants.

I am not funny at parties, but I'm good with the leftovers.
I have a sense for lids and their jars wearing label-glue residue.
When I am in love I am good with the laundry,
         bad about eyes on the road.

But December is not an accident waiting to happen,
                              it is the ditch.
                              We have already rolled.

I am trying to show there is nothing outcast about you.
I will armpit your hands for warmth. I will flare the dark,
I will splint and carry you through when you need it.

NUMBER LOVE, MY TAXES

Like a wrapped gift I had put off opening because the shake of it
said *I got right answers in me.* And I have been holding the map
in a fog so thick I can't see the length of my arm.
So this Cosmo quiz of income I'm counting on to make sense of
how we were never married, but I dream more than I sleep now.
Of how the fire alarm went off for twenty minutes at midnight,
hungry for a nine-volt, and hitting it with a broom handle
felt like shaking a baby.

My neighbor drives his kids four hours one way
to see their mom and she will still be locked up for years.
Someone abandons a wheelchair in the snow in front
of my house and somebody else shovels a bent path around it.
When they test my blood they ask *have you ever exchanged sex
for drugs or money or something that you needed?*
There must be a write off in all of this.

In the number of boxelder bugs trapped against storm-windows,
in the growing mole on my left breast, in the way a woman
puts her hot tongue to it long enough that I forget
my grandfather's melanoma, my Aunt Barb's mastectomy,
in who claims each of us and how they do it, how the tattoo
won't come off, how we are so many dependents,
how one headlight will do for now.

We expect a tear-away check in the mail some weeks
toward summer, those of us who didn't stack enough
in the black. I recycle the magazines wearing strangers'
names that I don't call to cancel because I am alone
enough already. And when the check does come the
watermark reads *leave this town, leave the state altogether*,
like a receipt stamped *no returns, no exchanges.*
You can't undo what you have done.

PALOMINO

After Mary Ruefle

Did you wait for hours at arrivals?
Did you curse when you got back in the car?
Did you eat an apple? Did you eat its core?
Did you drive to Mexico out of spite?
Did you get beat up in the water and left for dead?
Did you get a flat? Did you have a spare?
Did you listen to *Rumours* on repeat?
Did you elaborate?
Did you think about stealing a horse?
How long did you stand by the barbed-wire fence
picking out the one you'd take?
Did you strip the bed? Did you tip the maid?
Did you imagine remembering a birthday
would be like an old kiss?
Did you measure twice and cut once?
Did you trespass like you used to?
Did you carry the cassette for years?
Have you quit sleeping in other people's clothes?
Did you go blind, just for a moment, in the floodlight?
Did you stop to taste the gravel in my driveway?
Can you smell the silence on my breath?

THE MOST ELEGANT WAY TO
WIN WAS TO QUIT

The most elegant way to win
was to quit.

She asked will you meet
me in the tunnel? I answered,
Nothing and yes.

▲▲▲

If stones began so wide
we had no sight
of their beginnings—

The name for
an always shrinking absence.
    [Parabolic, Asymptotic]
I don't know;
    [Walking at the bottom of a canyon—]

The thing that I know
is the absence will keep shrinking.

▲▲▲

I spent the night in a cave.
I watched a man accidentally
catch a manta ray.
None of this is metaphor.

▲▲▲

Later a cop pulled me over
and let me go
saying no one is ever honest.

You know there is seclusion in truth-telling.
And such restraint.

PURPOSE IS THE BODY AND THE UN-BODY

My war could be a silent one
dressed in hooded vestments,
violent only in a quick vow
of refusal:

> *My rage will be my own and held*
> *warm against my chest. Will not be*
> *spoken for. Will be chanted hand*
> *in hand with joy.*

Fight strips the delicate sacredness
from ending. Paints you in colors.
Leaves you half-dead.

Let light cut a hole in the roof,
stillness dig a tunnel to the safe house.
Silence holds you like two boxers
in love, swinging at each other.
    It won't desert you when you need a war.

NO COLLAR

at least we have a river to go to
everyone erupting at the same time

number the secrets you are keeping
set a place at the table for each

a wishbone left to get a little more brittle
shuffled deck with a dog-eared ace

this emerging spring, a gas station
would that a final draft meant anything more

no news like a graveyard shift
and the minimum wage stayed put

what luck we have, keep it dry
the sweet gap left by a baby tooth

May Day coming brother swim to me
singing prison songs loud as a rail yard

IN THE BELLY OF THE HORSE

In the belly of the horse, in the timber hull,
they left one guard to sleep through the siege
folded with clemency into himself. Among many,

one telling is this: the unwitting pacifist,
a boy beekeeper lost in the Greek dreamhills
of his nightmind. The body in its heaviness

that pulls him out of the war like wet clothes
and drowning, like being hauled back onboard
with a gasp, limp and dripping, hefted down

to the bilge by strong arms. Do we carry
some residual hibernation in us that says,

go dormant beneath floorboards? Is it fair
to say there are fights I wouldn't want to win?

My brother trains horses to be unafraid
after neglect. For hours he rubs a halter
against his Arabian's jaw until the straps

are closer to a comfort. He told me
he could train a goat or even a chicken,
anything with desire and memory.

He's not my real brother. It doesn't matter.
In the field I hold a coffee can that he gradually
empties of carrots and crumbling biscuits.

He holds a clicker, the sound of oars in their
locks at sea. The horse holds a belly of fight.
We are far from either shore.

Still that grave littoral pull of body sleep-sinking.
The night I forfeited my August wall and its coolness
for a tent in the yard. On my own, turning again
one number older (and incidentally asleep).

The meteor shower went on pummeling;
how that barrage had blanket-weight.

I have come to know self-subterfuge as kindness.
The mythical knowing part of you yields in being
so stern, asks only if you need to bring a pillow, says

you can crawl back into the belly when you wake
to aloneness, discomfort, cold cowardice, mistrust.

SPIT VALVE HELLO

The late evening ash of forest fire
dandruffs the whole mingling backyard
and even at introduction I can't meet anyone new.

    Two men named Mackenzie,
    Lita with the eyes and posture
    of someone cruel from college,
    Madison or Morgan as blonde
    as a Maura that I used to know
    with small teeth, both of them.

I imagine holding a handful of teeth
like smooth white pills or beads,
rolling them through my fingers—
some nervous monk with a rosary.

A guy with his shirt on inside out
speaks at me about himself while I try
to count the number of teeth in my mouth
by touching my tongue to the back of each one.

Inside my mouth, I'm in eighth grade.
When they took off my braces I played
the trumpet a little better, but only a little.
They gave the surface of my teeth back to me
slick, almost slimy, having been away for years.

SUNDAY POLARIZED LENSES

Nothing looks nice on this couch.

Even uncles sodden in the ubiquity of always almost getting divorced.

But the nice thing about bringing the fruit salad is that you can put mango in it and leave out all the shitty fruits.

Fantasizing through an hour of names for a future DJ self leaves me where it always has—Drugdealer Boyfriend.

I'm told they are very very upper middle class, or maybe lower upper class.

One of everything on a doubled paper plate is really the last thing anyone has ever wanted.

More is more of the melted coleslaw that "still in love with Carl" sounds like.

I miss the petulant teenage apathy and resentment of being told to put on the pastel sweater and get in the car, we'll be outside.

Someone's not-wife (mine) is swept off her feet by someone else's father.

Evidently there will be skeet shooting tomorrow for those interested.

If only you, they, all watched more porn.

My own rented window is decorated from outside the house with the dried pointillist blood of a self-jealous robin.

The flashiest part of me gets off on guilt.

What can't be monogrammed?

Honestly, who?

ORANGE GROVE AND A VIEW OF THE PACIFIC

Wings inside a window frame.
The dish towel that held a bird
humming in my hands, Lily
keeping the chair steady.

Lily in a belly shirt before
one of us took it off.
This used to be a dress,
she said, I made it.

Lily's hair falls in the way
famous people move
their bodies.

From the guest room I
can hear the ocean
gasp. Sunscreen and salt
smell. My name sounds like
yes, sounds like a lost dog.

A YEAR OR TWO

I want very quiet, moneyed pain.
Not to be borrowing enough for bail
and waiting for the tow pound
attendant to unlock the gate.

He suggests you stop by a gas station
to get rid of the empties before
you get pulled over again.
You didn't get pulled over in the first place.

If we get out of East Missoula
in the next year or two
I'll give my anger over
to self-help and sweepstakes.

I'll kick the ass of the boyfriend
that you are far too good for,
then take up Zumba and Pilates.

I won't talk about getting dumped
in a trailer park anymore, begging.

I will lament that my grave plot
is not in the shade,
that my daughter's training wheels
are loose and rattling,
that the cat has a cancerous
growth just beneath its jaw.

Some dark July, when the tomatoes in
my overwatered garden split open,
only then will I blame myself, wonder
if I ever deserved organic anything.

I will fall to my knees
and break whatever delicate
chain I've worn around my neck
for years. I will think of us
at twenty-five, everyone we know
swimming in desire and resentment.

How did we make it out?
How will things have gone
just right enough that the godforsaken
4 A.M. phone call can't be for me.

LITTLE RECTANGULAR EARTHS

On Fourth of July in the 90s
I was desperate for a glowstick.
I mean, I knew we were supposed
to be in it for the fire sky, for the
red glare. We all knew, even before
the skyline lost both front teeth.
Floods Hill carpeted in bare legs
and Tupperware and cops mostly
not caring about open containers.

I had a thing for aliens then,
the lemon-lime egghead tapering
to a pointed chin. I was in it for
the genderlessness of their power
and deep space and truth revealed
in cornfields. Wanted three bucks
so I could bite through a fluorescent
necklace and spit light from my insides,
as neon as I knew them to be.

WHAT I LOATHE IN OTHERS I LIKE IN YOU

on the bedroom floor of fondness
facedown like a boyskin rug if I was one
carpet parted by my face bones in bad rough tufts
this is an adult moment in ways prostrate

you in the nosebleeds can't see, but trust that
this breath against the earthpull moves just enough
to feel the un-undone alloy button of my jeans
against what bone is there

the adult part would've been sleep-hungry
or having not sent the text about tequila
doing modified pushups on Sunday afternoon
knowing how none of this is worth mention

instead immodestly seeking some homely
cause for a clap on the back or towel snap
cut nails just skimming where I cannot reach
until under my shirt is everywhere electric

and then lying turned to standing
when I wanted to stop saying I so much
I thought so cleverly of the seeing parts
how I break every gaze that tries to hold me
where my nose breaks the surface of Narcissus Pond

you who put your feet to our friendship
or strip your clothes to the floor of it solitary
you have accounted for my failing and
drawn mustaches on my self-serious sleep
forgiven and forgiven about me

HEARD EACH OF US

when I heard you were gone to the desert
I lifted my half-drunk half-jar of wine
   over my head and tipped it.

just enough burgundy to be like the sea
in my eyes, that sharp. glass turned body warm
in my hand. one of the many extremities.

in a miles-long cellphone stretch,
the last thing you had said was gone.

  [When I am alone out there
  can I call to you?]

  my answer was no.
  don't call out for anyone.
  that's the point :

    how you forget the selfish sound
    of each of us.

I kept the jeans because they'd been new
and washed them. stains like dark vinegar,
but only the smell of their cedar drawer hiding place.
     said it was blood when I wore them once.
     said I gave my spleen to coyotes for the winter
     and they left a howling pond in me.

THE DIFFERENCE BETWEEN OASIS AND MIRAGE

People three degrees from me keep dying—
    from heatstroke walking the length of the Nile,
    in an avalanche (not as symbol but fact),
    standing in a heap of belongings thrown from a window
    when the body's no longer a home.

At a dinner party the hostess has drunk
enough wine to ask things like,
would you say that you're bisexual?
and *did you hear about the woman
who pulled over on Reserve and shot herself?*
Road flares like Roman candles,
the unbroken side window
an agua fresca fountain
running down the glass all day.

I keep breaking out, which is death only in that
I spend cumulative hours in front of the mirror.
Aren't we too old for this? Face says no.
Face holds indignant color where I've pinched it.
During sex, Emma tells me she likes it
when my hair is in my face—
I don't know how to take that.

In the bathroom it's morning.
I push my grown-out bangs around,
drop my chin and flip all of my hair into my face.
Then shake it a little and I get what she means—
it looks like I'm wearing a wig.

A month into my new job
my client stops taking his meds,
wants to ride this sickness out:
illness like it's a gelding, saddled and lame.
No side effects, though. Only effects.

He is trying to let this life go quick.
       I used to run everyday, he says, *I used to be undetectable.*

I repeat this aloud at home in the blue-dark kitchen.
Undetectable.   I stare into the fridge.
Undetectable.   I've forgotten what I'm hungry for.
Undetectable.   I have the thought that I am crazy.
Is this how it begins, with voices?

When Sadie wants me to talk her down
about her writing, I know to leave my phone
behind the seat of my truck and leave the truck
parked three blocks away.
Or lock my phone in the freezer.
Or throw it deep into the snow. This is how
we guard our ambient frequencies from the feds.
Her eyes heard a helicopter today and keep blinking.

We pace farther from the truck until
she tells me she's changed all the names
and left half of it out but stays afraid
for the thirsty bodies on the long border walk.

I am gripping her shoulders in an alley.
I am saying *don't let your life go undocumented in fear.*
No one has to know it was you who left water in the desert.
No one has to know that everything you write is true.

And I am not convinced and I don't know how to lie well.
But I know we've got animals in us like a house on fire.
They smell the smoke and they're digging at the doorframe.

ASTEROID RECOVERY

At the moment of impact, my brother said he felt nothing, he felt himself to be nothing, a curl of smoke from some extinguishment, the last of the species of himself, caught in the very moment of extinction. The cupboards of his clapboard chest shook enough to shatter their earthenware to the floor, and then the shards shook more. He is still quaking. He says there is no awake. At the moment of impact, a seismic shift split the sea, tide after tide so high his rupture. Whitecaps to batter the firmament, their fists to the punching bag sky, his fist blotting the sea from his eye. And nothing of himself, and everything taken away. At the moment of impact, his eclipse stayed dark. Leaning all his weight against a sun that strains to rise for him, like trapping torment shame behind a closet door though it pounds to be let out. The buoyant wisp of you, the unsettled dust of your body, that last wandering animal, typhoon beating and beating a nameless shore that is your every regret, you, pinprick light years away, shelves stripped bare, darkness blanket around shoulders. What of your dominion does not grieve with you?

WHAT IF THE DROUGHT STAYED

what if the drought stayed
and smudged us into smoke marks
licking white walls hungry

in some dirty daytime eden
beer was anyway cheaper than water

we kissed our books, unfolded them in our laps

what if I stayed and droughted you

became left handed
inscribed distance on what is not strange

smaller and smaller mysteries
deft utensil jasmine bites, sips
leave the wisteria, eat the air around it

when the rain comes it will be nothing

like the cold morning wait
wind shutting the door
ambivalent alarms set early

a tremor loud enough
to see the bay bridge ripple

A DEER MISTAKEN FOR A STATUE OF A DEER

There are deer in the suburbs
who know they don't belong there
and know they can't leave

After the time for flight
(and deer aren't fighters to begin with)
we get still and wait for
a change or an end—

I keep thinking that
I will die with my eyes open

And how in the city I am afraid
to leave the laundromat and how
I don't remember if I ever
put your black bra in the dryer—

When I was a hunter
I was never even a hunter then—

UPLAND HONEST

Every time we hike this hill
I end up ravenous, but gradually.

The pitch picks up as you describe
the ugly daylight moon
and the ring one of your friends
has given to another.
I tell you my new secretary
broke off her engagement for a woman
and, without breaking stride, you ask if it was me.

There are tacit ways we talk
about why we are not together
when we are together—
    We go into nature without other company,
    without a map or jacket, so that when
    I am cold I have to say that I am cold.
    We survey an entire town in miniature
    until *house* becomes a game the rest are playing.
    We call the in-between season profane,
    when half the trees are summer
    and half the trees play dead.

In single file, one of us is only a voice,
the other a pillar of salt.

My sock works hard at a blister.
The tamaracks haven't gone yellow,
though they threaten it like a pop quiz,
like something we've studied and forgotten.

We splay out on the bald hilltop,
close our eyes to the roiling sky.
My belly hunger-moans when
you lean your head against it—
ferocious, even the softest part of me.

THIS PARTICULAR SOLVENT

What exactly did you think you were going to get
out of a bowl of saltwater taffy?

Less a kind of sad? Less neighbor-sad?
Less street-sign-sad?

More a thought of the sea?

Go walk by moving water
was a prescription.

Take evening primrose oil
for the tenderness.

Every high-water mark, every low tide.

Daytime moon, what do you run from?

WITH HOLDING HANDS

Passing at the fish market, how brief
and broadly this came to stand
for the other side of a wall,
made it iridescent shimmering
irrefutable.

I don't want to touch
any more than to stand us beside
the winnower, her chaff
in our hair like snow if it could
bloom.

HAWK LIKE A STEEPLE

Sitting at the crest of Waterworks Hill
we decided we'd never get married.
I spread my arms to say *just this*.
You'd already left every home for me.

It was the most Quaker wedding,
simple, you and me in our coats
looking south over a new April
stranger town. Held a branch
behind your back like a bone,
ate strands of each other's hair—
no ring or witness. Rainless sky.

Our mothers want us to be mothers
and your father, who has been so dead,
is not dead to me. I tell him quietly
that I won't have you be anyone's wife.
Silence can't help but sing the coal trains
in their couplings through the valley.

BEYOND TASK AND FUTURE, ENDLESSLY WORTHY

After Joanna Klink

tonight I wish I had a god
to light the warm lamp
between here and what *here* is worth

setting out bread and blood for supper

because I have no kind of dominion
the blue spruce falls and falls and falls
in my mind it is nothing but falling

MUSEUM FEAR

this body of howling same|same desert silent darkness language
     of symbol & object & logic
I tried to hollow it out
  until the absence flooded

    I want to taste the fruits I've read about
    I want to kiss the part of you that speaks
    I want not to draw so near to anger
    I want the guard to hold my hand
      as we gather pieces of a broken thing

  that I will be asked
to stand in the corner
with my pockets turned out

    that I have touched
something irreplaceable and fractured it

      that what I never stole
    will still be found on me unexplained

IN THE PAINT

i.

I have called it *"don't respond"*
    wanted the part that walks through the desert still
a waver in the air each step

cactus like a hot stove
    out of reach pocket knife and tylenol
wanted to sit on the coal train tracks in January thaw
                                  or the pipeline trucks

    you know

I'm taking a different girl to basketball games this year
      it's like that

like the undead space jam website
    and that mythical space jordan
        fool on the poster on my closed closet door
                                  til way too old

way too long to be trying to fuck with *don't respond*

difference between a bull and a steer
how the power steering went out
     and it can't waver can't be fixed so stiff
upper lips two of us

ii.

Each close call totemic
a very evil eye worn a worn away button
   on yarn on a neck that is
               these wanders made it through protected

clever matchbook a little burning bush for a good time
   called cheaters never win quitters never prosper

stay close to this trigger as it's pulled *white hat*
   slow with unwavering draw

ghost of no remorse sketched in cloud shadow like cow hide

hindsight hubris
hindsight hardball years

come back and go to sleep *white hat*
   and where your undershirt unravels
         we will mend it

SOLITARY TASTING

At the grocery I mistake you for a twin of you,
with bare arms cold in the dairy.

I know who you cook dinner for.
I know what they like to eat.
And some tower of melons,
some cereal box wall in me,
denies a cart full for them.

A trending piece told me my life
would never be the same knowing:

    The filigree of flat parsley
    points more sharply
    than cilantro's curve.

What absent difference, now that I know.

Still, if you hand me a yam
and hand me a sweet potato
all you have made is a thief.

The longer I undiscern your body,
like an eclipse watched in a shoebox,
the more it seems as if this twin of you
would also press me against the kitchen counter,
borrow my shirt for an interview,
betray very little to the houseguests,
grow something red and sweet and bitter in the garden.

The twin of you, who is becoming more the real you,
turns away, leans the cart into motion.
A manager announces a cold cut special.
An automated mist crisps the vegetables.

SUPPER CONVERSATION

Roils like a washing machine
behind closed doors.
Rolls over in its death trick, more
the slower and slower sink trap.
Callous as a windchill
but the amber itself, the aging.
A ghost's hooved foot beneath the sheet.

▲▲▲

When the rest are thanksgiving
slip me exclusively exceeding profanities.
Big hands. A hare tied up in the bushes.
The true lensmaker who started smoke—
caught noon in unfocused ice.
I'm out twenty miles past Don't Fall
into the Fire, sculling the pond.

▲▲▲

Walked home in boots to save
the fare, row and row of orchard.
To have been excused, to have had
excuse: no.
My bandana oak tree like licking the ice
to claim it, like pissing in the street.
Gaslights hissing for the end of shift,
that by the bodies overhead this one
who wants to see can see.

INESCAPABLE LUCK

You, reckless hope of a town.
And my mother's dinner whistle,
and the shirt I stained mulberry,
with me bloodied in it
at the bottom of a tree.

The way fear and justice
cinched together at the knee
could run the three-legged race
and win.

Just enough streetlamp
to unknow a sidewalk place,
to lose one's feet beneath them,
to pass my own father at night
and recognize only his breathing.

This practicum of a day
we wake without worry,
without wandering away.

My basic anchor sound,
garage doors churning down.

RICOCHET

a starvation economy of joy is not inherent

                                            in everyone, it dawns on me

                                                    a little literal sun

put me in small white rooms

                                        windowless, this new racquet habit

I will go at it

alone

                              prefer an opponent known over unknown

the high ceiling what it sees

                          this animal builds itself a cage of accomplishment

and real cold doesn't speak with a zero-sum tongue

                                    when I tried to describe it over the phone

thought I'd stubbed my toes but this, just frostbite moving slow

                                    couldn't remember what I'd kicked so hard

                                        because I hadn't kicked anything

remember being a kid kicked in the stomach by a boy
I thought was my friend
if not for something so plain, would've kept thinking it

think it in buried parts still
the broken little hawk I found after school

YOU, THE UNDERSIGNED

surrender   bequeath   betroth

    your skin pressed
    ferocious marks of your name

places you have never been never wanted to go to
or leave from
    [mother's house | driver's seat |
            a town called Truth or Consequences]

alive page alibies you
alibies you deep for keeping

       know that in our knowing I will lie and lie
in weight in volume in uncalibrated symbol
[skinny dog | avalanche]
                       I will lie until it's true

undersigned, I say jump
you say
      how have I ever done anything but jump
agree
there is no breath of yours that is yours

and this incentive creep toward the tongue
   that keeps you safe
                 [the sour of it | swearword | manta ray | excuse]

   understudy
I can feed you lines to school play embarrassment
   wrote them with you in mind
wrote you all at once in undeceit

agree and I will grease you up
         beg no rest   take what's left
                  the slanted circumstances of being

launder all the money   bed sheets
scrub satellites   whole swaths of sky clean
   drown drunk for you
              [the river | the hot tub | the pacified Atlantic]

write your palm so it is read by kerosene in a night
            you will never know

RIPARIAN COUNTY

Once when I sat by the tracks on lunch break
the Empire Builder, running late, kicked up
some shred of a green bottle broken over its
rails like a christened ship. The glass barely
caught me beneath the eye, but it cut enough to bleed.
My boss clocked me out when I got back, wrote
bleeding face by my name, so I went to the river.

They came around the bend, ripples at their waists
wading the incongruous current, bare-breasted,
bare as a parking lot. I knew their faces
from a photograph buried in my wallet: you and I
had climbed a water tower to see the city behind us,
your brother (wrapped in secrets of his own) told us
to press closer together to fit the bridge in the frame, too.

The twins of us here hold hands in the river,
their hair longer than it's ever been. What am I to do
but pry off my boots, slide the folded picture
from its hiding place and hold it out of the water's reach?

In the current, in the middle of town, in disbelief I call out,
"I still keep this!" The worn image thrust out in front of me
like some boarding papers, like some permission.
The twin of me comes close, minnows around our ankles,
takes the hat from my head and puts it on her own,
sun making plain my face. "I keep it, too," she says.
Her voice is the sound of my message machine
if my message machine was in love.

The twin of you takes my chin in her wet hands, turns
my cheek to look at the gash. She presses her thumb to
the cut and my nerves howl a train track through my skin.

Of course she draws my blood across
her own face, an imitation wound.
Of course it is the sign for *even now we hurt the same.*
But I've forgotten how your talking sounds,
so the twin of you says nothing. Wades toward the riverbank
like stepping out of a skirt and leaving it on the floor.

REMEMBER DRIVING TO SALT LAKE CITY

in the night
in January
in my Volvo
    88 Volvo
    the love of my life
through Craters of the Moon
and Monida
    which is the front half of *Montana*
    and the front half of *Idaho* put together
    permanent population of two
past the Continental Divide
    which is how NPR reports the weather here
        winds east of the continental divide—
        west of the divide warmer
how I fell over stretching my butt muscles in the gas station bathroom
how the brother-in-law we went to see is no longer your brother
how I ask you now to tell me long distance
              I am still family

the sun came up in Utah
    with your eyes closed
the sun came up far from anyone's home
    frost fields and red hills

snow tires with road salt
hawk like a steeple

you remember waking up in Salt Lake City
you remember me undoing your seatbelt in the driveway
how there was no undoing then

AUXILIARY FILE FOR NOT-BRIAN

I quit my job, but gave enough notice
that on the day before my last day,
I opened my office door
to a room of two dozen balloons,
each rigged with a miniature light inside.
    Lights like little pills pulsing,
    changing colors
        against the one-time cleaned carpet,
    pills pulsing blue and red and green
    suspended from the metal brackets
        that hold up particle board ceiling tiles.

And I went for a walk on my lunch break,
and got to eat a red velvet cupcake
before eating my actual hummus lunch.
Pieces of construction paper taped to my wall
each sparkle their one glitter glue letter,
saying
    t h a n k y o u
    exclamation point.
And some of the glitter glue dripped down
    onto the baseboard,
        but not onto the leased gray carpet.

When one of my clients called to say
he gave 30 days notice on his apartment,
he asked if we would help
    with a new deposit
    and first month's rent,
and I told him it depends
    on the budget
    and on the rent.

He asks me to send him some craigslists
about two bedrooms when I have time,
and I say, *Brian,*
    the thing is
    tomorrow is my last day.
    But there'll be a new case manager, soon.
He says, *that's so fucked,*
what am I supposed to do.
    He says, *that's so gay*
        and I say, *yeah that's so gay,*

because it's Montana
and because we are
and because it is.

And his name isn't Brian,
because of how I have to keep
the file cabinet locked,
because of the virus and not

what it means
but what it meant
when it was the ghostmaker.

His name isn't Brian, it isn't anything
I can take with me,
except that at intake
I was faxing his papers to the clinic
    or from the clinic,
and I saw his birth certificate.

Not-Brian, we were born in the same hospital.

You and me,
    a few years apart,
        twelve hundred miles from here.
Not-Brian this is something to behold,
folded between labs and paystubs.
Let me take this knowing when I go.

CLOSING COSTS

There is a stretch of rail in the wetlands
where the power on the train cuts out
and the whole behemoth coasts,
humid and tepid. The children
go quiet. I am going to the house
where I was a child. I am going to
where deer ate lawns at night, lost,
where I tried to keep a raccoon as a pet,
where I am asked to turn my pockets out.
The train slides back into its electric pull.
A mile out, in a pile of reeds some storm of
grease smoke says, *impossible*, the swamp on fire.

SOME DAYS

Some days I want to use *muggle* as a slur. I want "you are not magic" to hold in it the kind of sting that burns all morning.

There's a way someone who's never been in a fistfight kinda wants that.

But what the city is good for: remembering the one climbable willow still mermaiding through the park in dusk.

The lifetime membership can be such a rip off but it just really depends.

And at some point that sucker of a stormtrooper must've realized those *were* the droids he was looking for. And then what?

A gaslight purpling the path.

The swim-up bartender calls it a Miami Vice—half piña colada / half daiquiri swirl.

The heroic part is that inside out underwear still works. This is no embarrassment.

The Morse code click of the burner before it lights. Whole milk hot chocolate, not for an occasion, just to drink.

It turns out the 40 degree river of alpine runoff is pleasure incarnate and she doesn't care if you strip down or not, if you put your face in, she's gonna keep running.

Get someone to touch your nerve endings.

With better eyes you can see the loose balloons even longer.

SAFELIGHT | COMPOSITE | STEREO

But how do you want to show up in the work?

        I ask, sitting between the two
        in the backseat in the parking lot,
        with a single-size cone of rocky road)—

        Like a ghost on film? Like a sunflare,
        or the pinhole or the light leak?
        I can underexpose our small touches,
        these belt loop giveaways.
        We're showing up so clearly.

Left says,   Right says,
   This sort of development   I have named myself
is no salt & silver. Don't call yourself   a lifetime of imagined sounds.
stop bath catalyst—be flesh to me.   This truth won't ask for defense.

                    . . . Also, your ice cream is dripping.

        I'll be the cold front, but warmer.
        You be brass scissors & their weight.

I'll be your steep blind curve.
You'll be my morning.

I'll be your warning bell.
& you be the same.

Left & right refused my abject object names.

& said,
No more convincing. Don't you see where you are?
Being sandwiched between us is so far from being eaten.
Our golden hour, steeped in alpenglow—
the blushing hills, all our lips flushed.
Every hitch needs a post for to bend around & bight.

Left says,   & Right,
    I will tie you to the bedpost,   I will leave you out in the rain,
    but in a nice way.   I will soak you through.

SCAVENGER

The three of us have begun keeping score,
    that the harvest is through
        that the oldest goats are slaughtered
            their hides salting in the greenhouse.

The days short enough that the farmhouse starts cold and
    visitor that I am
hefting an ax is no chore.
My arms full at the door
I see transparencies of myself in the double glass
storm window, as sweatered
and American and convinced of oncoming warmth
as the plaid November catalogues arriving

    with their two names and this address, pernicious.

The winter cribbage tally sheet has those names
    and me abbreviated, the thing of my name:

                        M | T | Mtn.

When I drive up 93 toward the farm,
　　toward the lake that hides the land around it,
　　the Mission Mountain range cracks the sky open.

I park in the driveway
　　　　　beneath grey so white　　it squeezes in
　　　　through spindle gaps　　in branches—
so close and unyielding
　　that the two father pines　　and the many maples
　　and the ornamental landscape trees　　do not life it up,
but wear that sky as a heavy collapse
caught in a moment of pause
from within the path to be devastated.

We three eat food and are in love. This is the easy way to say
there are stores beneath the floor.
　　　　Potatoes and shallots,
　　　　　　hard-necked garlic streaked purple,
　　　　　　jars beside jars, themselves
　　　　each staving globes of suction.
Preservation, a guardian hunger.

　　In the evening I whisper to the boiled beet,
　　　　like a naked organ in my flushed hand:
　　　　　　　　You are ground blood,
　　　　　　　　you are new born,
　　　　　　　　you have never been nothing—

thawfruit seedflower greenstart rootbulb handpull shedscrub mouthsweet
and again.

At the holiday table I say my gratitude
is a warm day and I am somewhat secret.

I go to stand beside the electric fence around the goats that are left
      and—animal—I ache to grab the charged wire,
      saliva iron in my mouth.

Later I am put to bed between the two and we buck and roll
      in the heat of not fucking and the sweat of the guests,
      how they know I belong to something
                              but don't know the to-whoms.

Still out by the grazed absence field,
I remember being photographed
      holding the tawny goat when he was a kid.
      His horn nubs burned down to the skull, to the not-grow.

They climb their doghouse shed, the goats.
Once, they got out and climbed my car.
I undo the power to the fence. I climb the shed like a kid.

A rash of lichen barnacled to the roof of sloping 1x4s.
    Sea dollars, if I give little white-capped hills to aquatic imagination.
    Jellyfish dried, flattened, and pressed within an atlas.
    Lichen the color of lamb's ear, but not the softness.
    The page of a book left in a steamy bathroom.

    Lichen like the squamous moon,
lichen like magazine photographs
                    from helicopters
                            over fertile tributaries
                                    as they dry.
    The newest colonies
only half of my smallest fingernail—a baby's breath of green
branching like tiny coral in the rooftop sea.

I am fascinated by the simplest rules:
that a full flush is all only ever luck,
that three of a kind is exponentially more valuable than a pair,
that the same turned card lives differently between us.
And the speed of a run and double run and double double run—
      coal black coal train stowaway run away.

An afternoon that Tracy goes to town
Margaret and I read *The Thistles in Sweden*
to each other, taking turns,
and find it altogether too close to this home.

    The story-woman wept
        when she tore down the curtains,
        but the real one just pinned them level.
    The story-woman had a child
        in her body and was made satisfied by it.
        This one spent the growing season
        with an abdomen of no baby, of "nobody's there."
            Sorrow in the no-child.

And crying in the rows of tomato pearls
beneath a broad-brimmed hat.
    When these conversations were so not mine to feel about—
        just held out my comfort hands in the field and,
    dazed from the summer sun,
    watched a bee bumble drunkenly
            among the blades of grass.

What fills the vacuum space when one is displaced
by a much smaller thing?
    The avalanche moves in me.

Iconography as it stands:
bison cut into wood : claim jumper claim jumper
dog-eared bedside : one million baby names
county line | rail line : place where you surround something
egg in the hen house : city pigeon,
                              a pencil through its neck and still alive
ledger : the dank erotics
            of a lover's gym clothes on the Sunday morning floor
February : shame muscles flexing in my mother's tight jaw

I think about you a lot now.
        You know this, in some way,
        even if you never come to exist.
I think about the insufferable things we ask of children.
    How I was born to make my mother happy,
        to make her into a mother
unlike her own—one whom we would not watch drown herself.
One who would not orphan her teenage daughter.
                        [Give me these pronouns for now, I need them.
                            It is always a *her*, it is always a doubling.]

And how I made myself secret.
The way 50 degree dusk will forever have me
                                walking home from middle school
                                uphill,
    how I was so unhappy then,
    how I lived outside my body,
            how I planned never to touch anyone.

When I thought about dying a lot, I was captivated by
self-immolating monks and Jains sweeping that uphill sidewalk
so as not to foot-crush a single worm beneath a leaf.
     The Jain death of rice   then water   then slow no-hunger
                                                  hallucination.
     I thought, I will keep this in my chest only.

And the other way I think about you—in phone call.
And in this thought, even now,
                    you are my grin.   You, small nothing.
I imagine it is Margaret on the phone,
so glad and afraid.
Or Tracy, or both of them, on speaker and I have a right thing to say.
I imagine you as their voices cracking because
                                        the wait has been a breaking too.

New abdomen growing.
                        Holding you when you are real,   if you are real,
saying you were the second stripe on a test that meant
more life in their house.
Once you are the "somebody's there," hold on hold on in there.

I will step away from the dinner table to take the call.
I will step into the pantry,   my own stores.
I will walk out to the shed,   I will climb on top of my own car.

I will let the cards fall. I will turn the power back on.
I will paint the room, I will build the crib.
I will love you hard,   I don't have to say it.

Will you grow here,
far enough out of town that the first time you hear a siren
it is a cowling caged-animal cry, bending through the hills?
     Will you have a name for me?
     Will you leave home angry?
     What part of you will be kept secret?

Listen, little somebody,
                         your mule is nothing stubborn.
It is the weary task for you,
                         that which will carry your weight
                         across unsteady ground
                         with certain hooves.

Believe that the bald-faced moon won't bluff,
that every drought has a brother monsoon,
that no shame is worth hiding,   it is theirs not yours.

I had gone to my mother's house alone, adult,
     to clean some things.

Before my walk to the uphill train station,
I let the door of the garage close for what seemed
    instinctively, if uncertainly,

                    to be the last time.

And in that slow mechanical shutting
a sigh was breathed between us,
our warm cavities equal in musty near-October.

            Appendix of a home,
            kites on the rafter shelf
            steeped in fumes of impatient idling.
            That exhaustion, held in beams,
            yielded soft with rot.

When the omnipotent gear began its overhead lurch
dust took on the breath smell of the dirt it had been,
    of spreading mulch over the dead dog,
    of closing the day's half used gallon of varnish,
    of car wax and Round-Up and fertilizer

                            put in their places
                            for a tidiness that is Mother's Day.

Will you do this with me?
                Shall we love them together?

You can call me the thing of my name,
and I can be small life
  and you can be large life   in their house.

                    Something I have never seen before.
                    This game half un-played.

I will stay in the guestroom if you'll have me.
   I will walk through walls to your crying sound.

Smallest smallest thing,
                         the avalanche asleep in you.

FORWARD FALLING DAYTIME

at sunrise I say light shut up
reset the dashboard clock while swerving
a travel mug rolling in the passenger footwell
that was not, it turns out, spill-proof

boulders in the rearview, like some molecular rushing
outran its invasive historic wearing away
pitted weed against parasite and hollowed out
my placeless worry

left my initials on a tabletop in Bozeman
scratched a rude mountain from a borrowed knife
sunrise road so steep the car curses me rhythmically

don't return my mother's calls in full
just that I am with my two friends at the edge of a mine
don't name them because I am far away from generosity
in general things are fine, the pit says hi

gas is still cheap and I'm afraid I won't be famous
cheesy cracker aftertaste stuck in my molars
what if I am known for nothing but forgetting to floss

we talk through a script about the end of humanity
reclamation and prairie grasses nine feet tall

possibility and integrity both a lessness
like towns called Phosphate, Racetrack, Anaconda, Opportunity
I want us to disappear, but all together so we won't be alone

OPEN THE BOX THAT HOLDS A FIRE

I made the rug my friend by looking at it so long
weaving and unweaving it with my eyes

the theologian says
your doubt is divine also
a door in the mountain

how it's easier to talk with my head bowed
orthodox for a religion that doesn't exist
have I come a long way

not progress nor distance, but it is both
bringing my chest close to another's chest
breathing and beating against it

a series of shut and unshut doors
trust turning with hinging tides

I have pilgrimmed
filled chambers with smoke in asking

quiet quiet night bell kneels on the floor
sleeping toward devotion

NOTES

The epigraph comes from the poem "To Elsie" by William Carlos Williams, which was published in his 1923 collection *Spring and All*.

"Elysian / Echo" contains a plum taken from Williams.

The boxers mentioned in "Southpaw Skin the Gloves" are Ray "Boom Boom" Mancini (American) and Kim Duk-Koo (South Korean). In 1982, the two fought at Caesars Palace, where Mancini won the bout by technical knockout in the 14th round. Immediately after the fight ended, Kim fell into a coma and died four days later. In the months following Kim's death his mother committed suicide, as did the bout's referee, Richard Green. This fight prompted the introduction of the standing eight-count call and a shift from 15-round to 12-round bouts. The coroner's children in this poem belong to the Williams poem, "Hic Jacet" from his collection, *The Tempers*.

The question asked in "Number Love, My Taxes," *have you ever exchanged sex for drugs or money or something that you needed?* is part of the standard counseling that accompanies a rapid HIV test.

"Palomino" owes a debt to Mary Ruefle's poem, "Merengue."

We begin in the city of Troy in the poem, "In the Belly of the Horse."

The term *undetectable* in "The Difference between Oasis and Mirage" refers to a suppressed HIV viral load, meaning that although it exists in the body, very few copies of the virus are present. This viral suppression makes HIV transmission very rare.

"Beyond Task and Future, Endlessly Worthy" responds to and takes its title from the poem, "On Falling (Blue Spruce)" by the brilliant Joanna Klink.

"In the Paint" references the following webpage: www.warnerbros.com/archive/spacejam/movie/jam.htm.

"Riparian County" was inspired by Stanley Kunitz's "Quinnapoxet."

The title of "Solitary Tasting" was adapted from an Allen Ginsberg line in "A Supermarket in California."

The poem "Some Days," includes the term *muggle*, which has been borrowed from J. K. Rowling's lexicon. The stormtrooper in this poem wandered over from the Mos Eisley Spaceport in *Star Wars: A New Hope* (1977).

In reading "Scavenger" it may be useful to know that cribbage is a card game traditionally for two players, but often modified for three, four, or more. "The Thistles in Sweden" is a short story by William Maxwell published in *The New Yorker* in 1976; the narrative of that story describes in detail the apartment of a couple struggling to conceive a child. The phrase *place where you surround something*, which appears in the iconography passage of "Scavenger," is a translation of the Salish name, *snyélmn*, for the region commonly referred to as St. Ignatius, Montana. As Rob Cheney of *The Missoulian* writes, "that name refers to a Salish hunting tactic, where men would build a temporary corral and chase deer or elk herds inside. In a single word, the name connotes a landmark, a food source, a harvesting method and a time of year when such tactics are effective."

"Open the Box That Holds a Fire" includes a line drawn from the title poem of Jean Valentine's collection, *Door in the Mountain*.

ACKNOWLEDGMENTS

Grateful acknowledgment to the editors and staff of the publications in which versions of these poems first appeared: *Barrow Street,* "The Book Is a Hungry Darkness"; *The Carolina Quarterly*, "Haymaker Barnburner"; *Colorado Review,* "Forward Falling Daytime"; *Cimarron Review,* "The Difference Between Oasis and Mirage"; *Devil's Lake,* "The Whole Water-Faced Auditorium"; *DMQ Review,* "Hawk Like a Steeple"; *Foglifter,* "Closing Costs," "Drive Thru," "On Being Told to Do Whatever I Want," and "Spit Valve Hello"; *Gris-Gris,* "Elysian / Echo"; *Guernica*, "Number Love, My Taxes"; *Hinchas de Poesía*, "In the Belly of the Horse," "No Collar," and "Beyond Task and Future, Endlessly Worthy"; *The Journal,* "Deadbolt Door Syndrome" and "Museum Fear"; *jubilat,* "Supper Conversation"; *LIT Magazine,* "In the Paint" and "Sunday Polarized Lenses"; *Little Patuxent Review,* "You, the Undersigned"; *Ninth Letter,* "Upland Honest"; *Pleiades*, "A Deer Mistaken for a Statue of a Deer" and "Riparian County"; *Prairie Schooner,* "Almanac Traction," "Asteroid Recovery," and "Southpaw Skin the Gloves"; *Sixth Finch*, "Some Days" and "What I Loathe in Others I Like in You"; *Smartish Pace*, "Scavenger" and "A Year or Two"; *The Southampton Review,* "Inescapable Luck," "Orange Grove and a View of the Pacific," "Palomino," and "Purpose Is the Body and the Un-Body"; *Spoon River Poetry Review,* "The Smallest Thaw"; *Up the Staircase Quarterly,* "Little Rectangular Earths"; *Witness,* "The Most Elegant Way to Win Was to Quit"; *Zone 3*, "What if the Drought Stayed" and "With Holding Hands." In addition, portions of this manuscript appear in the digital chapbook *Thin Fire*, published by BOAAT Press in 2018.

I sincerely appreciate the support of the University of Montana, the University of Denver, the Idyllwild Arts Fellowship, and the Virginia Center for the Creative Arts. These institutions provided me with time, space, resources, and community that made this book possible.

Brenda Shaughnessy, thank you for reading, thank you for writing, thank you. My gratitude to the staff of the University of Iowa Press—James McCoy, Gemma de Choisy, Charlotte Wright, Karen Copp, and Susan Hill Newton—for ushering me through the publishing process.

Deepest thanks always to Joanna Klink, Prageeta Sharma, Karen Volkman, Ed Skoog, Sherwin Bitsui, Jean Valentine, Bin Ramke, and Eleni Sikélianòs.

Huge gratitude to Caylin Capra-Thomas, Mackenzie Cole, Jules Ohman, Rachel Mindell, Philip Schaefer, Allison Linville, and all of my other invaluable readers who spent time with these poems as they developed. My heartfelt appreciation to Sarah Hill for always listening. My love and thankfulness to Madison Unsworth for keeping me nourished and warm, cheering me on, and keeping my boat afloat.

My heart for Roman and Tanner Pizzani, and Isaac Preiss; I am always here. Emma Quaytman, you are everywhere in this book, you are everywhere in my life, you are everywhere in my heart, always, my favorite vintage trinket. Thanks and love to my mom, to my dad, to Becca and to Jamie. Love to everyone in these pages and to the valley that held me, blanketed in cloud and smoke and sun.

IOWA POETRY PRIZE AND EDWIN FORD PIPER POETRY AWARD WINNERS

1987 Elton Glaser, *Tropical Depressions*

Michael Pettit, *Cardinal Points*

1988 Bill Knott, *Outremer*

Mary Ruefle, *The Adamant*

1989 Conrad Hilberry, *Sorting the Smoke*

Terese Svoboda, *Laughing Africa*

1990 Philip Dacey, *Night Shift at the Crucifix Factory*

Lynda Hull, *Star Ledger*

1991 Greg Pape, *Sunflower Facing the Sun*

Walter Pavlich, *Running near the End of the World*

1992 Lola Haskins, *Hunger*

Katherine Soniat, *A Shared Life*

1993 Tom Andrews, *The Hemophiliac's Motorcycle*

Michael Heffernan, *Love's Answer*

John Wood, *In Primary Light*

1994 James McKean, *Tree of Heaven*

Bin Ramke, *Massacre of the Innocents*

Ed Roberson, *Voices Cast Out to Talk Us In*

1995 Ralph Burns, *Swamp Candles*

Maureen Seaton, *Furious Cooking*

1996 Pamela Alexander, *Inland*

Gary Gildner, *The Bunker in the Parsley Fields*

John Wood, *The Gates of the Elect Kingdom*